# AFRICA
## World Continents Series

• • • • • • • • • • • • • • • • • • •

Written by David McAleese and Irene Evagelelis

## GRADES 5 - 8
### Reading Levels 3 - 4

**Classroom Complete Press**
P.O. Box 19729
San Diego, CA 92159
Tel: 1-800-663-3609 | Fax: 1-800-663-3608
Email: service@classroomcompletepress.com

www.classroomcompletepress.com

ISBN-13: 978-1-55319-311-1
ISBN-10: 1-55319-311-3
© 2007

### Permission to Reproduce

# Critical Thinking Skills

## Africa

| Skills For Critical Thinking | Reading Comprehension | | | | |
| --- | --- | --- | --- | --- | --- |
| | Location | Place | Human & Environment Interactions | Movement | Regions |
| **LEVEL 1 Knowledge**<br>• Match<br>• Show or Label<br>• List Information<br>• Recall Details (5Ws + H)<br>• Find Information | ✓<br>✓<br>✓<br>✓<br>✓ | ✓<br><br>✓<br>✓<br>✓ | ✓<br><br>✓<br>✓<br>✓ | ✓<br><br>✓<br>✓<br>✓ | ✓<br><br>✓<br>✓<br>✓ |
| **LEVEL 2 Comprehension**<br>• Describe & Compare<br>• Summarize<br>• Explain<br>• Select | ✓<br>✓ | ✓<br><br><br>✓ | ✓<br><br>✓ | ✓<br><br>✓<br>✓ | ✓<br>✓<br><br>✓ |
| **LEVEL 3 Application**<br>• Organize Information<br>• Interview<br>• Apply | ✓<br><br>✓ | ✓ | ✓ | ✓<br>✓<br>✓ | ✓<br>✓<br>✓ |
| **LEVEL 4 Analysis**<br>• Conclude<br>• Analyze | | ✓ | ✓<br>✓ | | ✓<br>✓ |
| **LEVEL 5 Synthesis**<br>• Design<br>• Create | | ✓ | ✓<br>✓ | ✓<br>✓ | ✓<br>✓ |
| **LEVEL 6 Evaluation**<br>• Evaluate<br>• Compare | ✓ | ✓<br>✓ | ✓<br>✓ | ✓ | ✓ |

*Based on Bloom's Taxonomy*

# Contents

**FREE!**

✔ **6 BONUS** *Activity Pages!* **Additional worksheets for your students**

- Go to our website: **www.classroomcompletepress.com/bonus**
- Enter item CC5753
- Enter pass code CC5753D

# Assessment Rubric

## Africa

Student's Name: _____  Assignment: _____  Level: _____

| | Level 1 | Level 2 | Level 3 | Level 4 |
|---|---|---|---|---|
| **Understanding Concepts** | Demonstrates a limited understanding of the concepts. Requires teacher intervention. | Demonstrates a basic understanding of the concepts. | Demonstrates a good understanding of the concepts. | Demonstrates a thorough understanding of the concepts. |
| **Response to the Text** | Expresses responses to the text with limited effectiveness, inconsistently supported by proof from the text | Expresses responses to the text with some effectiveness, supported by some proof from the text | Expresses responses to the text with appropriate skills, supported with appropriate proof | Expresses thorough and complete responses to the text, supported by concise and effective proof from the text |
| **Analysis & Application of Concepts** | Interprets and applies various concepts in the text with few, unrelated details and incorrect analysis | Interprets and applies various concepts in the text with some detail, but with some inconsistent analysis | Interprets and applies various concepts in the text with appropriate detail and analysis | Effectively interprets and applies various concepts in the text with consistent, clear and effective detail and analysis |

STRENGTHS:

WEAKNESSES:

NEXT STEPS:

# Teacher Guide

*Our resource has been created for ease of use by both* ***TEACHERS*** *and* ***STUDENTS*** *alike.*

## Introduction

This resource provides ready-to-use information and activities for remedial students in grades five to eight. Written to grade and using simplified language and vocabulary, geography concepts are presented in a way that makes them more accessible to students and easier to understand. Comprised of reading passages, student activities and mini posters, our resource can be used effectively for whole-class, small group and independent work.

## How Is Our Resource Organized?

### STUDENT HANDOUTS

**Reading passages** and **activities** (*in the form of reproducible worksheets*) make up the majority of our resource. The reading passages present important grade-appropriate information and concepts related to the topic. Included in each passage are one or more embedded questions that ensure students are actually reading and understanding the content.

For each reading passage there are **BEFORE YOU READ** activities and **AFTER YOU READ** activities. As with the reading passages, the related activities are written using a remedial level of language.

- The BEFORE YOU READ activities prepare students for reading by setting a purpose for reading. They stimulate background knowledge and experience, and guide students to make connections between what they know and what they will learn. Important concepts and vocabulary from the chapters are also presented.

- The AFTER YOU READ activities check students' comprehension of the concepts presented in the reading passage and extend their learning. Students are asked to give thoughtful consideration of the reading passage through creative and evaluative short-answer questions, research, and extension activities.

The **Assessment Rubric** (*page 4*) is a useful tool for evaluating students' responses to many of the activities in our resource. The **Comprehension Quiz** (*page 31*) can be used for either a follow-up review or assessment at the completion of the unit.

### PICTURE CUES

This resource contains three main types of pages, each with a different purpose and use. A **Picture Cue** at the top of each page shows, at a glance, what the page is for.

 **Teacher Guide**
- Information and tools for the teacher

 **Student Handout**
- Reproducible worksheets and activities

 **Easy Marking™ Answer Key**
- Answers for student activities

### EASY MARKING™ ANSWER KEY

Marking students' worksheets is fast and easy with this **Answer Key**. Answers are listed in columns – just line up the column with its corresponding worksheet, as shown, and see how every question matches up with its answer!

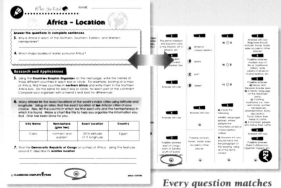

*Every question matches up with its answer!*

# Bloom's Taxonomy

## *Our resource is an effective tool for any* **GEOGRAPHY PROGRAM**.

## Bloom's Taxonomy* for Reading Comprehension

The activities in our resource engage and build the full range of thinking skills that are essential for students' reading comprehension and understanding of important geography concepts. Based on the six levels of thinking in Bloom's Taxonomy, and using language at a remedial level, information and questions are given that challenge students to not only recall what they have read, but move beyond this to understand the text and concepts through higher-order thinking. By using higher-order skills of application, analysis, synthesis and evaluation, students become active readers, drawing more meaning from the text, attaining a greater understanding of concepts, and applying and extending their learning in more sophisticated ways.

Our resource, therefore, is an effective tool for any Geography program. Whether it is used in whole or in part, or adapted to meet individual student needs, our resource provides teachers with essential information and questions to ask, inspiring students' interest, creativity, and promoting meaningful learning.

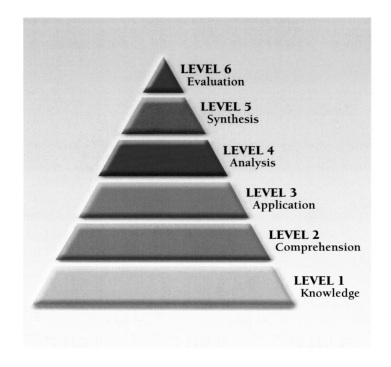

**LEVEL 6** Evaluation
**LEVEL 5** Synthesis
**LEVEL 4** Analysis
**LEVEL 3** Application
**LEVEL 2** Comprehension
**LEVEL 1** Knowledge

**BLOOM'S TAXONOMY:
6 LEVELS OF THINKING**

*\*Bloom's Taxonomy is a widely used tool by educators for classifying learning objectives, and is based on the work of Benjamin Bloom.*

# Vocabulary

- Hemisphere • prime meridian • connect • latitude • longitude • climate • Equator • absolute • exact • relative
- location • links • continent • northerly • tropical • rainforest • extremes • moderate • humid • plains • herds
- wildlife • mountainous • peninsula • feature • ocean • passenger • place • route • transportation • valleys
- savannah • coast • interaction • dependent • independent • unique • desert • physical • characteristic • vegetation
- region • exploration • port • harbor • agriculture • grassland • endangered species • rhinoceros • trade
- population • environment • positive • negative • pollution • game reserve • extinction • ancient • monument
- irrigate • preserve • adapt • pollution • responsible • resources • habitats • survive • harsh • poaching • remote
- forestry • mining • vehicles • industry • products • electricity • rural • urban • communication • helicopters
- tourists • scattered • canal • movement • automobile • impassable • camel • temperament • ancestors • ancient
- region • languages • fertile • pharaoh • giraffe • geographer • temple • Egyptian • sandstorm

 Before You Read

# Africa – Location

**1. Which word matches the definition? Color the arrow that points to the correct word.** You may use an atlas or a dictionary to help.

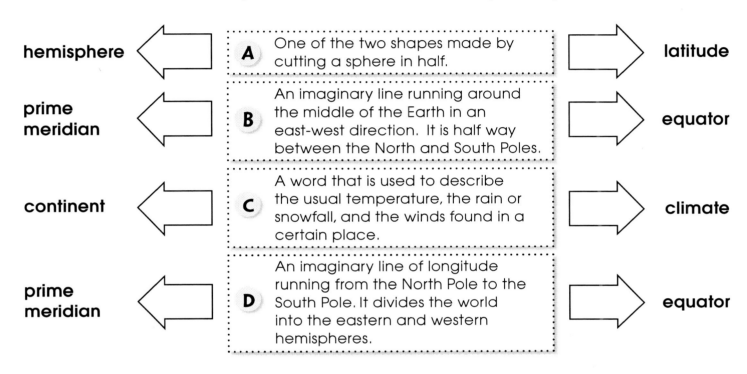

hemisphere ⇐ **A** One of the two shapes made by cutting a sphere in half. ⇒ latitude

prime meridian ⇐ **B** An imaginary line running around the middle of the Earth in an east-west direction. It is half way between the North and South Poles. ⇒ equator

continent ⇐ **C** A word that is used to describe the usual temperature, the rain or snowfall, and the winds found in a certain place. ⇒ climate

prime meridian ⇐ **D** An imaginary line of longitude running from the North Pole to the South Pole. It divides the world into the eastern and western hemispheres. ⇒ equator

**2.** On the map, color Africa in **green**.
Show the prime meridian as a **red line**.
Show the equator as a **purple line**.

# Africa - Location

**W**e can describe **location** in two ways.  If we describe the **absolute location** of a place, we describe exactly where it is found by looking at where lines of **latitude** and **longitude** cross.  When we describe its **relative location**, we describe the things around it and the things that connect it to other places.

Africa is the world's second largest continent.  It is so large that parts of it are in both the eastern and western hemispheres, and both of the northern and southern hemispheres!  Both the **Equator** and the **prime meridian** pass through Africa, meeting at a point just south of Ghana, in the Gulf of Guinea.  Its eastern boundary is near 50°E longitude, and its western boundary is near 17°W longitude, with almost 5,000 miles between these two points!  It is also approximately 5,000 miles from its most northerly point to its most southerly point.  Because it is so large, it is very difficult to give its absolute location.  It is easier to describe Africa's relative location by looking at those features and places around it.

Africa is like a large island, surrounded by several large bodies of water.  The Atlantic Ocean lies to the west, the Indian Ocean to the east, and the Mediterranean Sea to the north.  These bodies of water provide **links** between Africa and the other continents.  Europe is to the north, Antarctica is to the south, and Asia is to the east.  Africa is linked to Asia at the Sinai Peninsula.

**STOP**

### Why is Africa like an island?

_____

_____

_____

Africa's huge size and location gives it many different, extreme **climates**.  In Africa we find both the Sahara Desert and the Kalahari Desert, each vast, dry, and hot.  Near the Equator are huge tropical rainforests, hot, wet, and humid, and full of wildlife.  There are also many areas of flat, hot plains through which herds of animals pass, and several mountainous regions throughout the continent.

# Africa – Location

---

1. **Circle** **T** if the statement is true or **F** if it is false.

| | T = True |
| | F = False |

**T** **F** **a)** Africa is the world's second largest continent.

**T** **F** **b)** The prime meridian does not pass through Africa.

**T** **F** **c)** The Atlantic Ocean lies to the east of Africa.

**T** **F** **d)** Europe is north of Africa.

**T** **F** **e)** Antarctica is to the south of Africa.

**T** **F** **f)** Africa is linked to Asia at the Panama Canal.

**T** **F** **g)** The Sahara is a rainforest in Africa.

---

2. **You be the teacher!** Someone has matched the word on the left to the definition on the right. Are they correct? If **yes**, mark it correct with a check mark in the box beside each. If **no**, write an **X** in the box and correct the work by drawing an arrow to the correct definition. You may use an atlas or a dictionary to help.

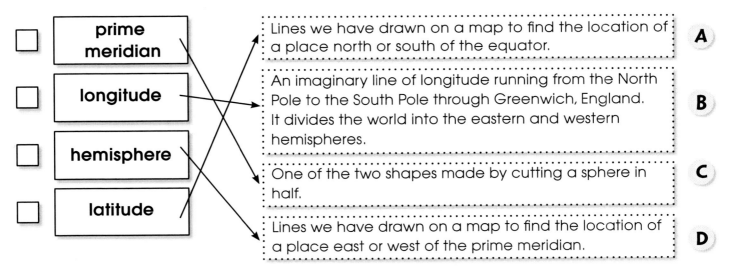

| ☐ prime meridian | Lines we have drawn on a map to find the location of a place north or south of the equator. | A |
| ☐ longitude | An imaginary line of longitude running from the North Pole to the South Pole through Greenwich, England. It divides the world into the eastern and western hemispheres. | B |
| ☐ hemisphere | One of the two shapes made by cutting a sphere in half. | C |
| ☐ latitude | Lines we have drawn on a map to find the location of a place east or west of the prime meridian. | D |

# Africa – Location

**Answer the questions in complete sentences.**

**3.** Why is Africa in each of the Northern, Southern, Eastern, and Western Hemispheres?

_____

**4.** Which major bodies of water surround Africa?

_____

## Research and Applications

**5.** Using the **Countries Graphic Organizer** on the next page, write the names of three different countries in each box or circle. For example, looking at a map of Africa, find three countries in **northern Africa** and write them in the Northern Africa box. Do the same for each box or circle, for each part of the continent. Compare your organizer with a friend's and look for differences.

**6.** Many atlases list the exact locations of the world's major cities using latitude and longitude. Using an atlas, find the exact location of **ten** African cities of your choice. Also, list the country in which we find each city and the hemisphere(s) in which it is found. Make a chart like this to help you organize the information you find. One has been done for you.

| City Name | Hemisphere (give two) | Exact Location | Country |
|-----------|----------------------|----------------|---------|
| Cairo | northern and eastern | 30°N latitude 31°E longitude | Egypt |

**7.** Find the **Democratic Republic of Congo** on a map of Africa. Using the features around it, describe its **relative location**.

_____

_____

# Countries Graphic Organizer

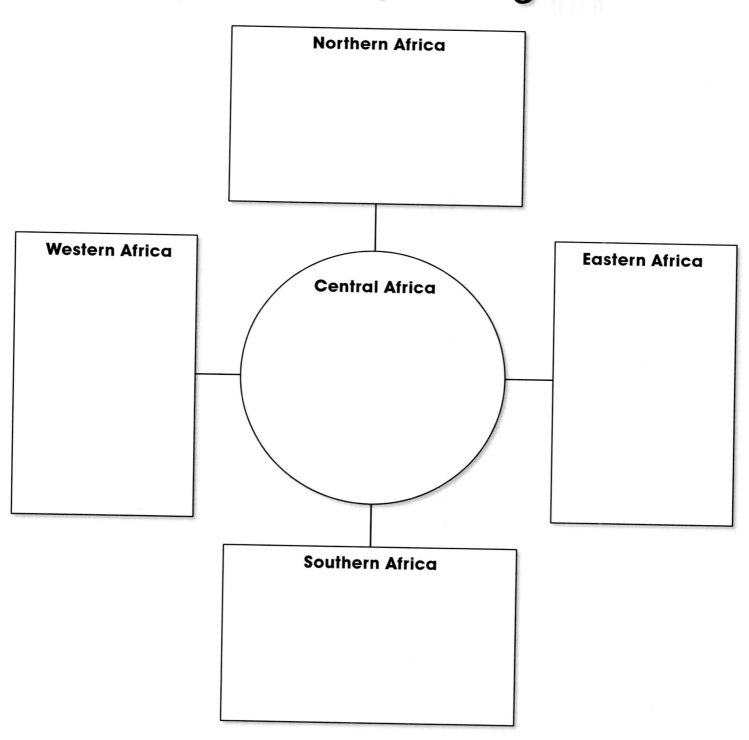

**Northern Africa**

**Western Africa**

**Central Africa**

**Eastern Africa**

**Southern Africa**

# Africa – Place

**1.** **Match the word on the left to its definition on the right. You may use an atlas or a dictionary to help.**

| port |

| desert |

| plains |

| physical characteristics |

> The features of a place that help us recognize and describe it. They may include mountains, plains, forests, deserts, or bodies of water.  **A**

> A flat, open area of land, mostly covered by grasses instead of trees.  **B**

> A large harbor where many ships come to drop off and pick up products to be delivered across the ocean. Passenger ships also use large ports.  **C**

> An area with very little rain and very little vegetation.  **D**

**2.** Make a list of those things that you **already know** about Africa using the following chart. You may also include some small illustrations if they help you express your ideas.

| Plants and Animals of Africa | Countries in Africa | The Landscape of Africa | The People of Africa |
|---|---|---|---|
|  |  |  |  |

# Africa – Place

**W**hich features make Africa **unique**? Perhaps it is the **wildlife** we find there. Maybe its **physical characteristics** make it unique. Perhaps it is the **people** of Africa, and where they have chosen to live, and the languages that they speak. Each of these features helps us better understand Africa and describe it as a **place**.

Africa is a **continent** of huge contrasts. While large cities can be found throughout the continent, some people continue to maintain their tribal customs and live as they have for thousands of years, preserving a unique way of life. Many people in Africa live near coastal areas, while others prefer the savanna regions, areas of grasslands and certain kinds of agriculture.

There are many important cities on all of Africa's ocean coasts. They developed there because they had easy **access** to transportation and **trade** with other continents. The ports of northern Africa make travel to Europe very easy. East African **ports** provide an easy **route** to Asia. The harbors of western Africa provide access to North America and western Europe. The Suez Canal in Egypt provides a short cut from the Mediterranean Sea to the Indian Ocean.

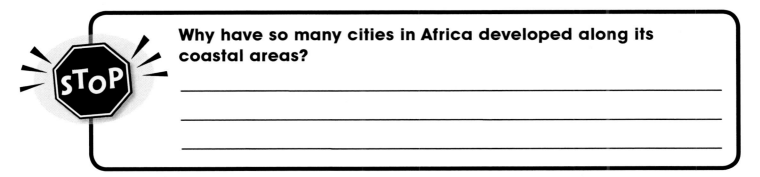

**Why have so many cities in Africa developed along its coastal areas?**

_____

_____

_____

The physical characteristics of Africa are many. There are huge rainforests at the Equator. There are vast plains in eastern Africa. There are tall mountains, deep valleys, and huge deserts in different parts of the continent. The world's largest desert, the Sahara, covers northern Africa like a hot, sandy blanket.

# Africa – Place

**1. Put a check mark (✔) next to the answer that is most correct.**

**a)  In which country would we find the Suez Canal?**
- ○ **A**   in the Sahara Desert
- ○ **B**   in western Europe
- ○ **C**   in South Africa
- ○ **D**   in Egypt

**b)  East African ports provide an easy route to _____.**
- ○ **A**   Asia and Antarctica
- ○ **B**   North America and western Europe
- ○ **C**   the Sahara Desert
- ○ **D**   the Indian Ocean

**c)  What is the name of the world's largest desert?**
- ○ **A**   Kalahari
- ○ **B**   Sonora
- ○ **C**   Gobi
- ○ **D**   Sahara

**2.    Read each of the examples below, and write a sentence describing how it helps preserve our environment.**

**a)** Circle those things that geographers use to describe **place**.

| | | | |
|---|---|---|---|
| **automobiles** | **ships** | **languages spoken** | **wildlife** |
| **where people live** | **mountains** | **physical characteristics** | **valleys** |

**b)** Using the words that you have circled, write a short paragraph describing what is meant by the word **place**. You may look back at the reading for ideas as well.

_____

_____

_____

_____

# Africa – Place

**Answer each question with a complete sentence.**

**3.** Why do many of Africa's important cities develop on Africa's ocean coasts?

_____

**4.** Why is Africa a continent of huge contrasts?

_____

## Research

**5.** Find out more about the **Masai** people of eastern Africa by conducting some simple research. Collect facts on their ways of life and complete a chart like the one below. Then, present your facts in a short brochure or on a poster. Illustrate your work.

| a) Where do the Masai live? | b) What language is spoken by the Masai? | c) Clothing? Food? | d) What are some Masai customs? |
|---|---|---|---|
|  |  |  |  |

**6.** Many of Africa's animals are **endangered species**. Research some of the endangered species of Africa, by finding how endangered it is and why, and its habitat. One has been started for you.

| Animal Species Name | How endangered is it? | Its habitat |
|---|---|---|
| black rhinoceros |  |  |
|  |  |  |

**7.** Many different **languages** are spoken in Africa, many within a single country! Find **ten** examples of different languages spoken, and name the country in which they are spoken. Complete a chart like the one below.

| Language | Spoken in which countries? |
|---|---|
|  |  |

# Human/Environment Interactions

**1.** **Complete each sentence with a word from the list. Use a dictionary to help you.**

| environment | monument | interaction | game reserve |

**a)** A _____ is a protected area where animals can live free from the threat of hunters and poachers.

**b)** A _____ is something created by people to mark a special event, the special deeds of a group or an individual, or to mark a place where someone is buried.

**c)** The word _____ describes all that surrounds us: the living things around us, the climate, the air we breathe, the water we drink, and the land we live on.

**d)** The way one thing acts on another is called an _____.

**2.** Read each of the examples below, and write as much information as you **already** know about the subject. You may write in complete sentences or in point form notes.

**WATER**
(Why do we need it?
 Why is it important?
 What is water pollution?)

**ENDANGERED SPECIES**
(What does endangered mean?
 Will they become extinct?
 How can we help?)

# Human/Environment Interactions

**E**very day, the things that people do affect their **environment**. While we work to protect **endangered** species, some people continue to kill them. Sometimes we harm the habitats of animals with pollution. When an environment is harsh or changing, people must often adapt to their environment to survive. Sometimes we might **dam** a river in order to provide more water for communities that need it. Learning about these issues is known as the study of human/environment **interactions**.

In Egypt, people have relied on the Nile River for thousands of years to provide them with the water they need to survive in the harsh desert conditions around them. The river water is used for drinking, washing, and watering crops. In the past, the Nile would flood its banks and **irrigate** the crops. In modern times a dam has been used to control the amount of water flowing through the country, providing water as it is needed. The first dam was built at Aswan in 1902, but was later replaced in the early 1970's by the Aswan High Dam. This dam blocked the flow of the river and created Lake Nasser behind it. Care was taken to preserve wildlife and ancient **monuments**. The ancient Egyptian Temple of Abu Simbel was taken apart and reassembled in a location away from the lake, preserving it as a national monument.

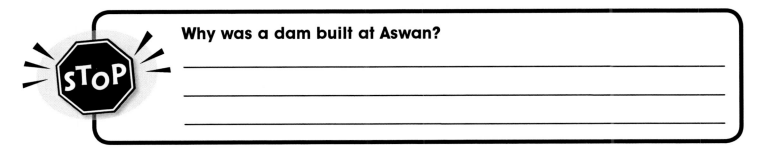

**Why was a dam built at Aswan?**

_____

_____

_____

Unfortunately, not all interactions between humans and their environment are positive. Throughout Africa, many animals are facing extinction because of **poaching**. For example, elephants are hunted for their tusks, and rhinoceroses are killed for their horns. Poachers sell the tusks as ivory, and the horns as medicine. Thankfully, many governments in Africa have acted to stop this poaching. They have made it against the law to hunt these animals, and have created **game reserves**, like the Masai Mara National Park in Kenya, to protect the endangered animals.

# Human/Environment Interactions

**1. Which word matches the definition?  Color the arrow that points to the correct word.  You may use either the reading or a dictionary to help find your answers.**

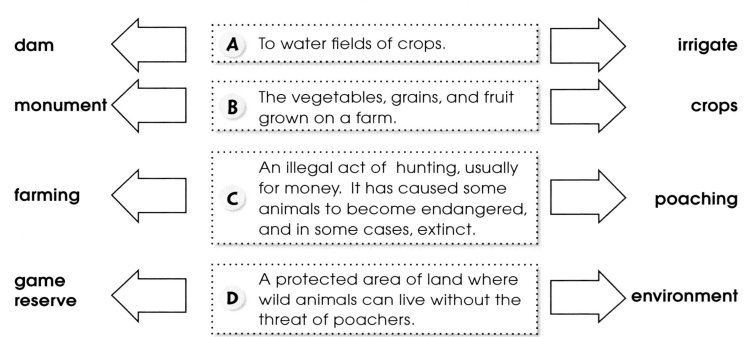

dam ⟵ **A** To water fields of crops. ⟶ irrigate

monument ⟵ **B** The vegetables, grains, and fruit grown on a farm. ⟶ crops

farming ⟵ **C** An illegal act of hunting, usually for money.  It has caused some animals to become endangered, and in some cases, extinct. ⟶ poaching

game reserve ⟵ **D** A protected area of land where wild animals can live without the threat of poachers. ⟶ environment

**2.** Circle **T** if the statement is true or **F** if it is false.

| T = True |
| F = False |

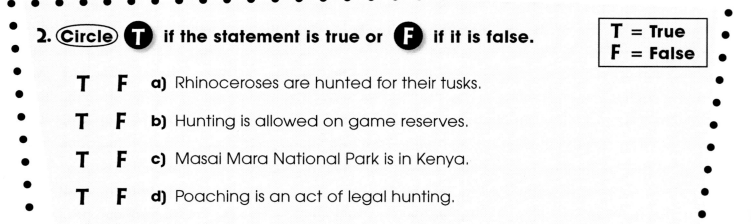

T  F  **a)** Rhinoceroses are hunted for their tusks.

T  F  **b)** Hunting is allowed on game reserves.

T  F  **c)** Masai Mara National Park is in Kenya.

T  F  **d)** Poaching is an act of legal hunting.

T  F  **e)** The Nile floods its banks and irrigates crops.

Africa CC5753

*After You Read*

# Human/Environment Interactions

**Answer each question with a complete sentence.**

**3.** Some human/environment interactions are negative. Why is poaching a negative interaction?

_____

**4.** Some human/environment interactions are positive. Why is a game reserve a positive interaction?

_____

## Research, Extensions and Applications

**5.** Find out more about the **Aswan High Dam** by conducting some simple research. Find answers to these questions and present them in a **poster** format. Illustrate your work and present it to your class.

**Why was the Aswan High Dam built?** • **How have countries used it to their benefit?**
**When was it built?** • **How much did it cost to build?** • **Which countries took part?**
**Which ancient Egyptian monuments had to be moved?**
**How were the ancient Egyptian monuments moved?**
**How has Lake Nasser changed the area around it?**

**6.** Locate a **game reserve** in Africa and create a **travel brochure** for it. Pretend that you are going to take your class on a safari to the reserve. What would you see? What kinds of animals are there? How would you travel there, inside the game reserve? What would you need to bring with you? Illustrate your brochure, and include as many facts as you can. You may wish to include a map of its location to help your class find it!

**7.** Many animals of Africa are endangered. Research two of them and complete the **Endangered Animal Organizer** on the next page. Follow the prompts inside the rectangles. When you have finished the rectangles, **evaluate just how close these two animals are to extinction**. The oval on the organizer represents extinction. On the bold arrows, place an **X** to show just how desperate the animal's future is. If the animal is very close to extinction, place the **X** close to the oval. If it is still not that close, then place the **X** farther away on the arrow from the oval.

# Endangered Animal Organizer

| **Endangered Animal and Facts** (How many are left, where they live, etc.) | **Endangered Animal and Facts** (How many are left, where they live, etc.) |
|---|---|

**Things Being Done to Protect It**

**Things Being Done to Protect It**

**EXTINCTION!**

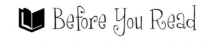 

# Africa – Movement

**1.** Think about your day.  How did you move from place to place?  How did you share your ideas with other people?  Make a list of the things you do for these each day.

_____

_____

_____

_____

**2. Match the word on the left to its definition on the right.  You may use an atlas or a dictionary to help.**

| urban | An area in the country or a remote area with few people, and less access to services, such as hospitals, shopping, offices, and recreation activities.  Many of these areas develop near a natural resource such as forestry, mining, or farming. | **A** |

| communication | The word used to describe how humans move themselves and other items from place to place. It includes the vehicles we use and the things they travel on (air, water, roads, etc.). | **B** |

| transportation | An area in a town or city, with a dense population, industry, and many services, such as hospitals, shopping, offices, and recreation activities. | **C** |

| rural | The sharing of ideas through many different ways, such as through speech, printed words, signals, sign language, and images. | **D** |

# Africa – Movement

**A**s **geographers** look at the Earth, they study movement, a word used to describe how people, ideas, and products move from place to place. In Africa, people travel to work, to school, or to **recreational** activities. Vehicles travel within and between countries and continents delivering the **products** that people use in their homes. People in Africa make telephone calls, write letters, watch TV, and surf the Internet looking for information. Radios and newspapers help spread news and opinions.

Many people have the false impression that most of Africa is wild and difficult to get to. In some cases this is true, because some desert, mountain, or rainforest regions are **impassable** by ground vehicles. In these **remote** or **rural** areas, traditional forms of **transportation** are used. You might see oxen pulling a cart. You might see someone riding a camel in a desert setting. However, camels are often used now to attract tourists rather than to provide daily transportation. Small airplanes and helicopters fly tourists into remote areas, four-wheel drive vehicles make passage through remote areas easier, and trains carry people to stations scattered throughout the continent.

In **urban** areas, people rely on many different forms of transportation. Trains help people and products get from place to place. Bicycles, cars, motorcycles, motor scooters, buses, and trucks are used each day. People in Africa also travel by plane or by ship. Africa's many coastal ports provide links to other continents. The Suez Canal in Egypt, allows ships to take a shortcut from the Mediterranean Sea to the Indian Ocean!

**STOP**

**On which forms of transportation do Africans rely?**

_____

_____

_____

NAME: _____

# Africa – Movement

1. **Circle** **T** if the statement is true or **F** if it is false.

| | | |
|---|---|---|
| | | **T = True** |
| | | **F = False** |

**T   F**   **a)** Africa is completely impassable, and people cannot travel through it.

**T   F**   **b)** Transportation is a word we use to describe movement involving vehicles.

**T   F**   **c)** The Suez Canal is a shortcut from the Mediterranean Sea to the Atlantic Ocean.

**T   F**   **d)** Small planes and helicopters often carry tourists into remote areas.

**T   F**   **e)** Africa has many radio stations and newspapers to help spread news and opinions.

**T   F**   **f)** Africa's many coastal ports provide links to other continents.

**T   F**   **g)** Traditional forms of transportation can be found in more remote and rural areas.

**T   F**   **h)** Four-wheel drive vehicles do not work in remote areas.

2. **How do you use these things for movement?  Explain in a few sentences giving examples of when and how you used them.**

telephone _____

_____

automobile _____

_____

school bus _____

_____

Internet _____

_____

# Africa – Movement

**Answer each question with a complete sentence.**

**3.** In what different ways do people communicate their ideas?

_____

_____

**4.** Airplanes are very important in Africa. Have you ever been on a plane? If yes, describe where you were going, and what the plane was like.

_____

_____

## Research and Applications

**5.** Traditional images of African deserts have people riding camels through the sand. Why are camels shown in this way? Research camels to find out why they are suited to travel in the desert. Think of these questions while conducting your research:

**How can camels go long distances without water?**

**How do a camel's hoofs help it move through the sand and rocky parts of the desert?**

**What is a camel's temperament (i.e., angry, calm, grouchy, tame)?**

**Why do camels spit?**

**Do people still ride camels from place to place?**

**What harness or saddle do you need to ride a camel?**

**What is a camel's value to people living in a desert climate?**

Present your findings as a **pamphlet** or a **poster** advertising what you have learned. Illustrate your work. Share your findings with the class.

**6.** While your family may have lived in your current home for a number of years, your **extended family** and **ancestors** probably came from a variety of different places, in a variety of different ways. Interview your parents to find out where your family originated, how and when they moved about, and how your immediate family came to live in your present home. Record your findings and share them with your class.

# Africa – Regions

**1.** A **region** is an area of land that can be described by the following things:

**a) size** (large or small) ⟶ [ ]

**b) changes over time** ⟶ [ ]

**c) physical characteristics**
(hills, valleys, rivers, etc.) ⟶ [ ]

**d) where, how, and why**
**people live there** ⟶ [ ]

Think of your school, pretending that its building, schoolyard, and nearby neighborhood is a region. How would you describe it? In the box beside each way of describing a region, give details about your school. Your teacher might need to help you or share your work with a partner.

**2. Using a dictionary, find the definitions of the following words.**

a) region _____

b) border _____

c) unique _____

d) ancient _____

# Africa – Regions

**G**eographers use the word **region** to describe an area of land. A region is described by the **features** that make it **unique**, and can be either small or large. Regions are often studied over time to see how they have changed. To understand a region, geographers look at a region's **physical characteristics**, where, how, and why people live in a certain area, and by the **languages** spoken there. Africa has many regions.

The Nile Valley is a well-known region in Africa because of its long history. The Nile is the longest river in the world, and has affected the lives of people, wildlife, and vegetation for thousands of years. Along either bank of the river is a rich, green, fertile strip of land. People have raised crops in this area for thousands of years, relying on the river to provide the water they need. Outside of this strip is a hot, dry desert. Along the river are modern towns and cities, as well as the ruins of ancient Egyptian society. In the ancient city of Luxor we find the temple of Karnak, and in Thebes we find the Valley of the Kings, known for its mummies of ancient pharaohs. A large dam can be found at Aswan, providing a basin of water that can be released when needed. Further south is the ancient monument of the pharaoh Rameses II at Abu Simbel.

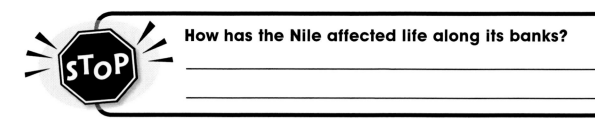

**How has the Nile affected life along its banks?**

_____

_____

One of Africa's most famous regions can be found along the **border** between Kenya and Tanzania. This area is known as the Serengeti Plains. It is a flat, grassy area filled with a variety of wildlife, such as giraffes, elephants, wildebeests, and lions. The Masai Mara National Reserve is one of many game **reserves** created to preserve the endangered animals that live there. In certain areas, mountains can be seen rising far in the distance. From Kenya's Amboseli National Park, an area in which the endangered black rhinoceros can still be found, visitors can see the snow capped peak of Mount Kilimanjaro to the south.

*After You Read*

# Africa – Regions

1. **Circle** **T** if the statement is true or **F** if it is false.

| | | |
|---|---|---|
| | | **T = True** |
| | | **F = False** |

**T    F    a)** The Valley of the Kings is found in Thebes.

**T    F    b)** The Temple at Karnak is in the ancient city of Luxor.

**T    F    c)** Geographers describe a region only by the language spoken there.

**T    F    d)** Mount Kilimanjaro is found south of Kenya's Amboseli National Park.

**T    F    e)** The word **region** is used to describe an area of land.

2. **Think of the regions mentioned in the reading. Match the region to each of its features using arrows. The first has been done for you.**

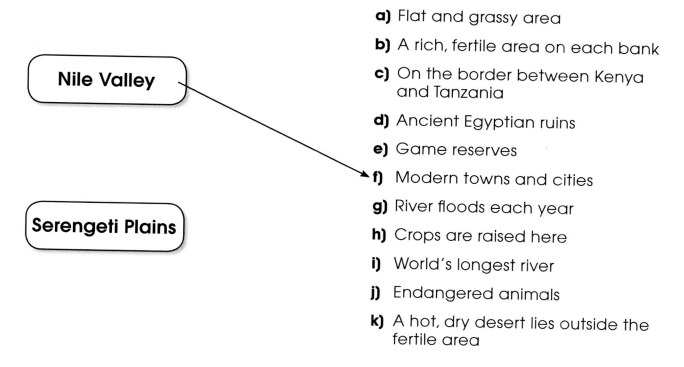

**Nile Valley**

**Serengeti Plains**

**a)** Flat and grassy area

**b)** A rich, fertile area on each bank

**c)** On the border between Kenya and Tanzania

**d)** Ancient Egyptian ruins

**e)** Game reserves

**f)** Modern towns and cities

**g)** River floods each year

**h)** Crops are raised here

**i)** World's longest river

**j)** Endangered animals

**k)** A hot, dry desert lies outside the fertile area

# After You Read 📖

# Africa – Regions

**Answer each question with a complete sentence.**

**3.** Be like a geographer!  Describe the Nile Valley region.

_____

**4.** Describe the Serengeti Plains.  What makes this region unique?

_____

## Research and Extensions

**5.** The **Sahara Desert** is a region that is constantly changing.  Sandstorms and winds reshape the surface of the sand each day.  However, did you know that the Sahara Desert is actually growing larger each and every year?  It is!  Conduct some simple research on the Sahara Desert and find answers to these questions:

   **Why is the Sahara Desert growing larger?**
   **How much does it grow each year?**
   **How has this affected the people who live near the desert?**

After you have collected your information, share it with your class.

**6.** Find an example of each of the following types of regions in Africa.  Use a physical or vegetation map of Africa to help you.

| Type of region | Found in this country | Name of region (if possible) |
|---|---|---|
| **savannah** (plains) | | |
| **mountain range** | | |
| **valley** | | |
| **desert** (not the Sahara) | | |

Highlight the type of region in the chart that most interests you.  Find out more about that region, and create a **travel booklet** for that area.  What would someone visiting that region see?  What would the weather be like?  Give as many details as you can.  Remember to illustrate your work.

NAME: _____

# Crossword Puzzle!

plains
desert
game reserve
absolute
continent
negative
transportation
endangered
Asia
rural
region
communication
contrasts
Nile Valley
links

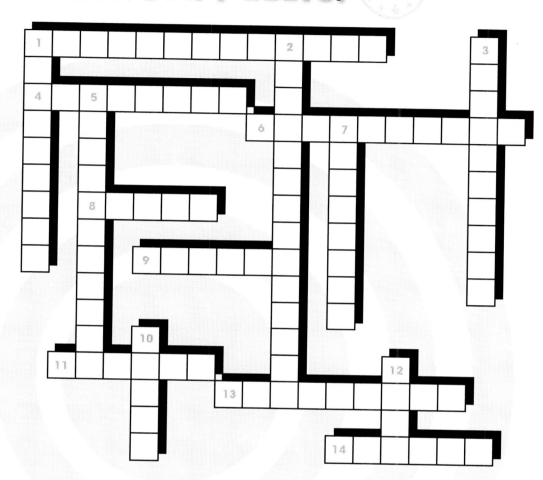

## Across

**1** Sharing of ideas through speech, sign language and printed words

**4** Poaching is an example of ____ human/environment interactions

**6** Many of Africa's animals are _____ species

**8** A remote area with few people

**9** The Saharah is a _____ in Africa

**11** A ____ can be described by the languages spoken there

**13** Africa is a continent of huge _____

**14** Flat, open areas of land covered mostly by grasses

## Down

**1** Africa is the world's second largest _____

**2** Movement involving vehicles

**3** The ____ _____ is a region known for its ancient Egyptian ruins

**5** Protected area where animals can live free of threats from humans

**7** It is difficult to describe Africa's _____ location

**10** Africa's coastal ports provide _____ to other continents

**12** Africa is linked to _____ at the Suez Canal

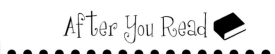

NAME: _____

# Word Search

**Find all of the words in the Word Search. Words may be horizontal, vertical, or diagonal. A few may even be backwards! Look carefully!**

| | | | |
|---|---|---|---|
| hemisphere | camel | interaction | trade |
| Africa | continent | poaching | Egypt |
| wildlife | rainforest | Suez Canal | endangered |
| region | plains | airports | irrigate |
| Serengeti | agriculture | climate | elephant |
| monument | unique | desert | Internet |
| Abu Simbel | Masai Mara | characteristics | oxen |

| q | e | u | q | i | n | u | w | f | w | i | l | d | l | i | f | e | c |
|---|---|---|---|---|---|---|---|---|---|---|---|---|---|---|---|---|---|
| a | p | o | a | c | h | i | n | g | s | d | f | g | h | n | m | n | h |
| r | a | i | n | f | o | r | e | s | t | h | v | g | h | t | m | d | a |
| z | x | c | c | v | b | n | m | a | s | d | f | g | l | e | h | a | r |
| o | p | i | l | v | m | a | s | a | i | m | a | r | a | r | x | n | a |
| a | f | r | i | c | a | e | f | v | d | s | h | a | n | a | g | g | c |
| o | g | e | m | v | g | f | d | d | d | d | d | b | a | c | f | e | t |
| c | i | g | a | r | r | v | r | f | r | r | g | u | c | t | v | r | e |
| o | r | i | t | a | i | r | p | o | r | t | s | s | z | i | v | e | r |
| n | f | o | e | s | c | c | g | j | n | v | r | i | e | o | d | d | i |
| t | a | n | f | s | u | s | d | e | t | h | g | m | u | n | t | b | s |
| i | y | r | d | j | l | c | o | d | e | n | a | b | s | a | n | a | t |
| n | n | p | o | r | t | d | d | w | w | h | n | e | f | f | e | f | i |
| e | e | l | e | w | u | w | g | t | e | b | b | l | b | b | m | e | c |
| n | a | a | g | y | r | p | n | r | t | t | f | d | h | l | u | t | s |
| t | x | i | d | x | e | a | e | g | y | p | t | a | s | e | n | a | d |
| b | o | n | p | l | h | h | b | e | f | f | d | o | w | w | o | g | x |
| z | z | s | d | p | p | j | k | s | e | b | c | d | x | f | m | i | g |
| q | r | s | e | s | h | q | w | d | r | c | h | g | t | e | j | r | l |
| m | l | l | i | h | d | d | a | g | x | f | t | u | q | f | n | r | e |
| m | e | m | o | d | d | r | s | s | e | r | e | n | g | e | t | i | m |
| d | e | s | e | r | t | e | b | i | n | t | e | r | n | e | t | u | a |
| h | e | j | k | g | b | n | p | o | r | r | g | e | o | g | r | a | c |

30

NAME: _____

# Comprehension Quiz

## Part A

Circle **T** if the statement is true or **F** if it is false.

| T = True |
|---|
| F = False |

**8**

T  F   **a)** Both the prime meridian and the equator pass through Africa.

T  F   **b)** Africa is like a giant island because it is surrounded by water.

T  F   **c)** People in Africa live in either traditional or more modern ways.

T  F   **d)** The Suez Canal provides a shortcut from the Indian Ocean to the Mediterranean Sea.

T  F   **e)** Game reserves provide protection for animals from poaching. The Aswan High Dam was built to help control the waters of the Nile River.

T  F   **f)** Latitude and longitude are used to find a place's relative location.

T  F   **g)** The word urban describes an area in the country or a remote area.

## Part B

**Label the map by doing the following:**

**1.** Show the following features on the map by writing the letter on the map in the correct location.

**6**

   **a)** Atlantic
   **b)** Europe
   **c)** Indian Ocean
   **d)** Atlantic Ocean
   **e)** Mediterranean Sea

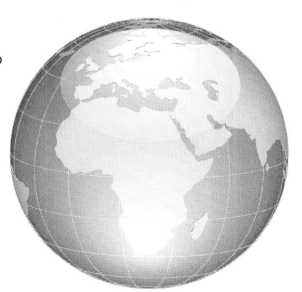

**2.** Color the prime meridian **red** and the equator **purple.**

**SUBTOTAL:**   **/14**

*After You Read* 📖

# Comprehension Quiz

## Part C

**Answer the questions in complete sentences.**

**1.** What is the difference between **absolute** location and **relative** location? As an example, describe Africa's relative location.

( 4 )

_____

_____

_____

**2.** How do we describe **place**?  Describe Africa as a place.

( 3 )

_____

_____

**3.** Describe what is meant by **human and environment interactions**. Explain how the poaching of animals is a negative interaction.

( 3 )

_____

_____

**4.** What do we mean by **movement** in geography?  Give one example of transportation and one of communication.

( 3 )

_____

_____

_____

**5.** What is a **region**?  Describe the Nile Valley as a region.

( 3 )

_____

_____

_____

**SUBTOTAL:**     **/16**

**3.**
Answers will vary
Response should include: travel, trade, easy access to other places

**4.**
Possible answers: modern way of life vs. traditional (tribal); wide variety of physical characteristics; etc.

**5.**
Possible answers:
**a)** Kenya and Tanzania border area
**b)** A Nilotic language (of the Nile basin area)
**c)** Clothing: traditional (i.e. men – red cloaks; women – neckpieces); ornamentation; body decoration
Food: follow their herds of cattle
**d)** A nomadic people who follow their cattle

**6.**
Answers will vary

**7.**
Possible answers: French (Morocco), Egyptian (Egypt), etc.

(15)

---

**1.**
**a)** Ⓒ D
**b)** Ⓐ B
**c)** Ⓐ D

**2.**
**a)** Circle the following:
wildlife, languages spoken, where people live, mountains, physical characteristics, valleys
**b)** Answers will vary; should follow the first paragraph of the reading, using all of the terms circled

(14)

---

**1.**
**A** physical characteristics
**B** plains
**C** port
**D** desert

**2.**
Answers will vary

(12)

Possible answers: travel, trade, easy access to other places

(13)

---

**3.**
The prime meridian and equator cross in the Atlantic off of Ghana, etc.

**4.**
Indian Ocean, Atlantic Ocean, Mediterranean Sea

**5.**
Answers will vary

**6.**
Answers will vary

**7.**
Possible answers: east of Congo, north of Zambia, south of Sudan, west of Uganda, etc.

(10)

---

Completely surrounded by several major bodies of water (i.e. Atlantic Ocean, Indian Ocean, etc.)

(8)

**1.**
**a)** T
**b)** F
**c)** F
**d)** T
**e)** T
**f)** F
**g)** F

**2.**
✗ prime meridian – **B**
✗ longitude – **D**
✗ hemisphere – **C**
✓ latitude – **A**

(9)

---

**1.**
**A** hemisphere
**B** equator
**C** climate
**D** prime meridian

**2.**
The prime meridian is the vertical line, the equator is horizontal. Africa is shaded.

(7)

**1.**
a) **F**
b) **T**
c) **F**
d) **T**
e) **T**
f) **T**
g) **T**
h) **F**

**2.** Answers will vary in complexity and detail

Possible answers:
trains
bicycles
cars
ships
airplanes
scooters
buses, etc.

**1.** Answers will vary

**2.**
**A** rural
**B** transportation
**C** urban
**D** communication

**3.** Possible answer: Illegal hunting for money that reduces the number of animals in a species, often to the point of extinction

**4.** Possible answers: Protects animals from poachers, extinction

**5.** Answers will vary in detail depending on resource used. Some possibilities: Built in late 1960s to control the flooding of the Nile, also generates electricity, has created more agricultural land; Abu Simbel was moved, cut apart, and reassembled, etc.

**6.** Answers will vary (many game reserves are found in eastern Africa)

**7.** Answers will vary

**1.**
**A** irrigate
**B** crops
**C** poaching
**D** game reserve

**2.**
a) **F**
b) **F**
c) **T**
d) **F**
e) **T**

**1.**
**a)** game reserve
**b)** monument
**c)** environment
**d)** interaction

**2.** Answers will vary, depending on prior knowledge

Possible answer: To regulate the flow of water down the Nile

**Across:**

1. communication
4. negative
6. endangered
8. rural
9. desert
11. region
13. contrasts
14. plains

**Down:**

1. continent
2. transportation
3. Nile Valley
5. game reserve
7. absolute
10. links
12. Asia

**3.** Answers may vary; Should reflect the information from question 2

**4.** Answers may vary; Should reflect the information from question 2

**5.** Answers will vary depending upon resources used

**6.** Answers will vary (i.e. desert: found in Namibia and Botswana; region's name is Kalahari)

**1.**
a) T
b) T
c) F
d) T
e) T

**2.**
**Nile Valley**
b, d, g, h, i, k

**Serengeti**
a, c, e, j

**1.** Answers will vary

Possible answers: Provides water for people, animals and crops

**2.**
Possible answers:
a) Area of land that has unique characteristics
b) A boundary line between countries
c) Distinct
d) Very old

**3.**
Possible answers:
e-mail
radio
television
Internet
telephone
cell phone
talk
letters

**4.** Answers will vary

**5.** Answers will vary in complexity and detail depending on the resource used. Possibilities: Produce little urine and allow body temperature to get quite high; walk on the front part of the hoof only, etc.

**6.** Answers will vary

## Part C

**1.** Possible answers:

Absolute – gives a place's exact location using latitude and longitude;

Relative – gives a place's location by describing the features around it, and the connections it has to other places;

Africa – south of Europe, west of the Indian Ocean, east of the Atlantic Ocean, south of the Mediterranean Sea

**2.** Possible answers:
mountains, plains, rivers, towns, cities

**3.** Possible answers:
How humans and the environment interact in both positive and negative ways;
Poaching – illegal hunting of animals for money, often drives a species to the point of extinction

**4.** Possible answers:
How people, ideas, and products are moved from place to place (i.e. plane, train, ship, bus, bicycle, e-mail, radio, television, Internet, telephone)

**5.** Possible answers:
Large or small area of land, described by its physical characteristics, vegetation, language;
Nile Valley – fertile region along river, desert outside of that, ancient ruins, Aswan High Dam

## Part A

a) **T**
b) **T**
c) **T**
d) **T**
e) **T**
f) **F**
g) **F**

## Part B

equator

Prime meridian

# Word Search Answers

# Africa
## World Location Map

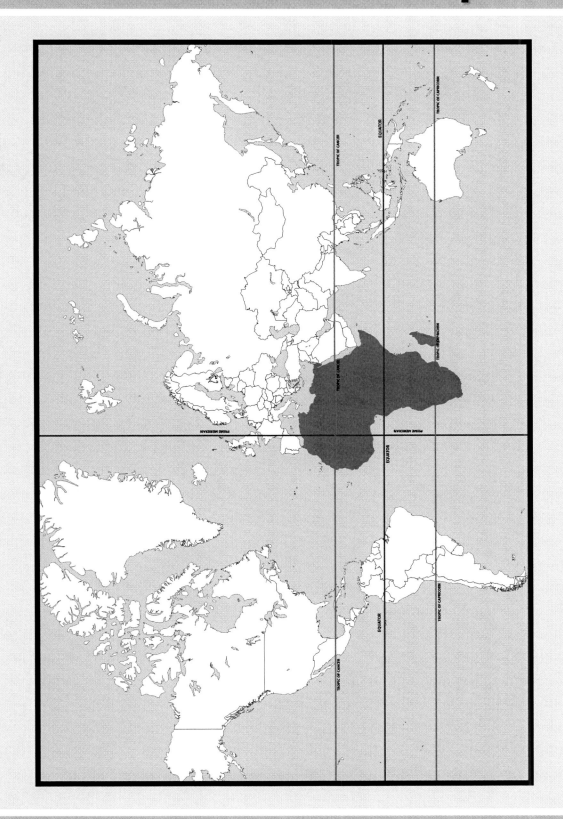

# Africa
# Globe View Map

# Africa
# Outline Map

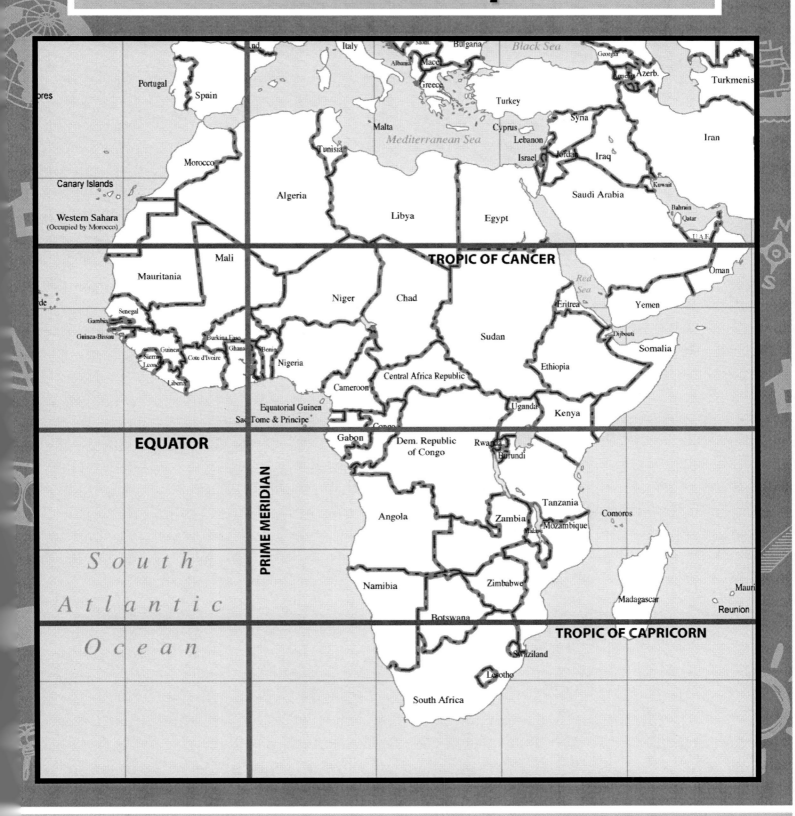

# Africa
# Physical Map

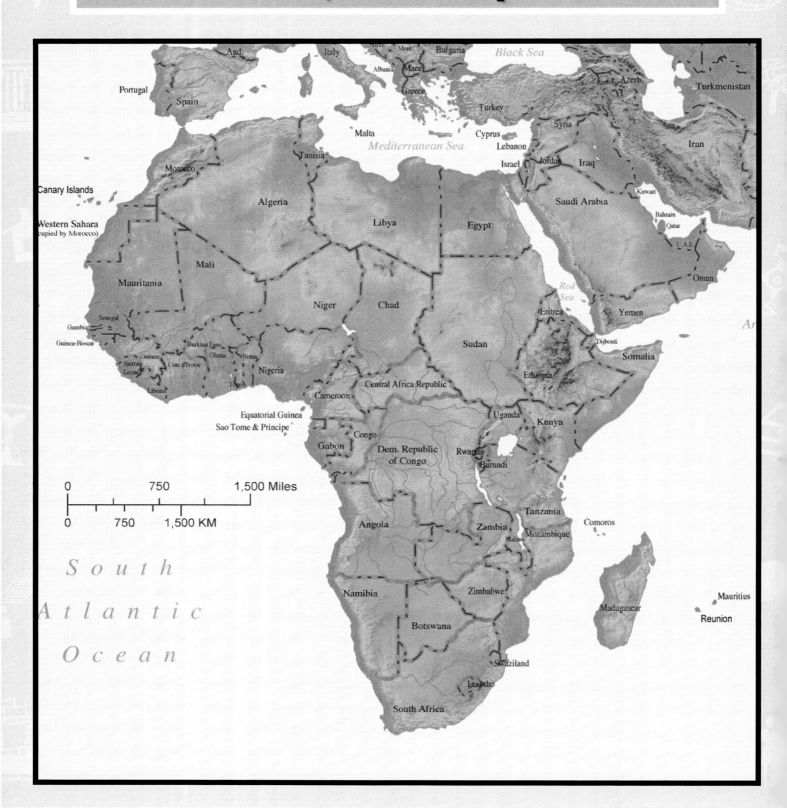

# Africa
# Major Population Map

Country
★ **National Capitals**
• Major City

# Africa
# Political Map

# Africa
# Transportation Map

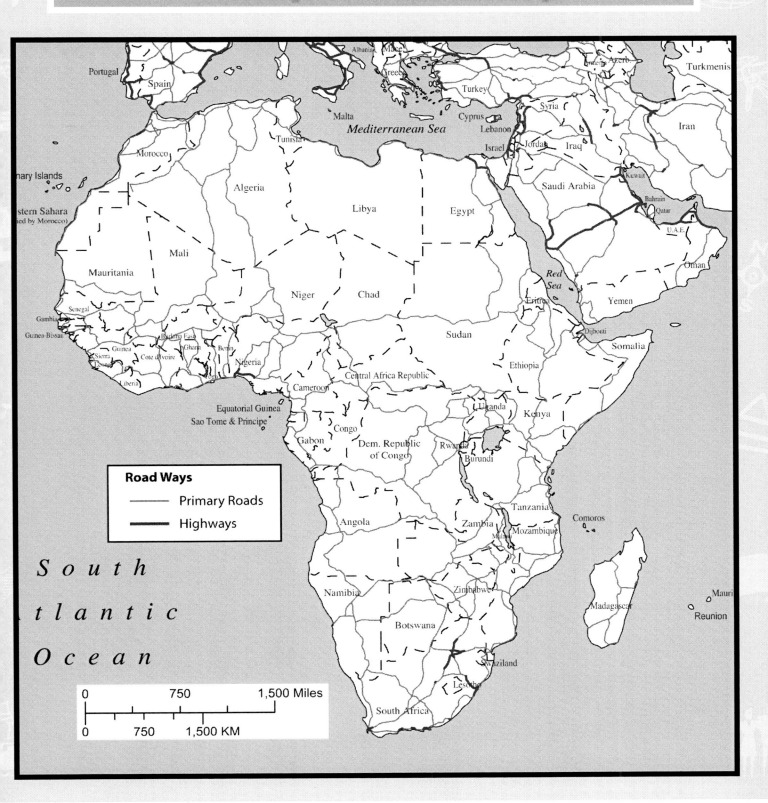

**Road Ways**

— Primary Roads

**—** Highways

*South Atlantic Ocean*

| 0 | | 750 | | 1,500 Miles |
|---|---|---|---|---|

| 0 | | 750 | | 1,500 KM |
|---|---|---|---|---|

Africa CC5753

# Africa
# Water Way Map

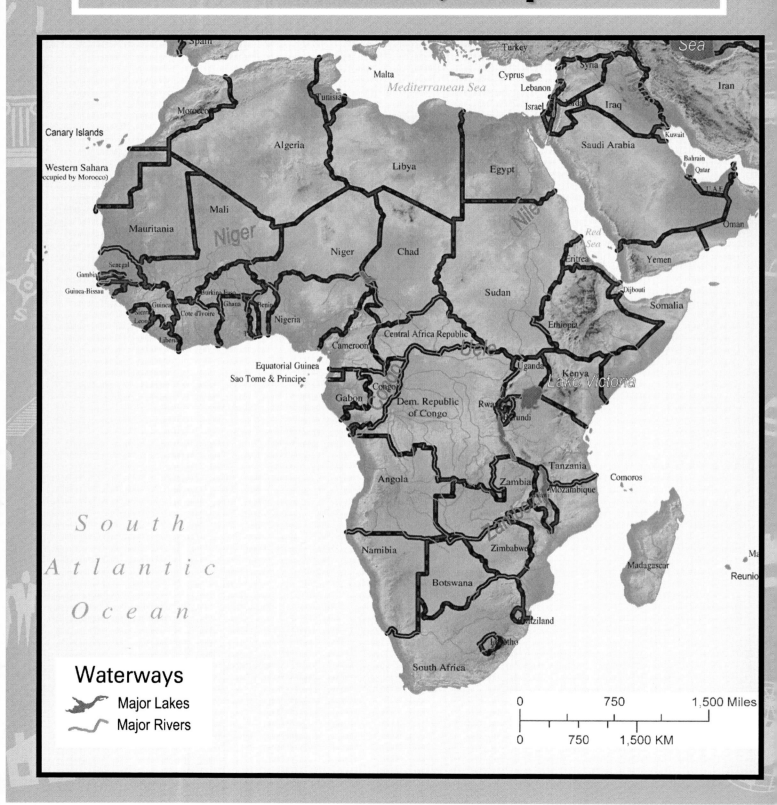

Waterways

Major Lakes
Major Rivers

| 0 | 750 | 1,500 Miles |
| 0 | 750 | 1,500 KM |

# Africa
## Continent Outline Map

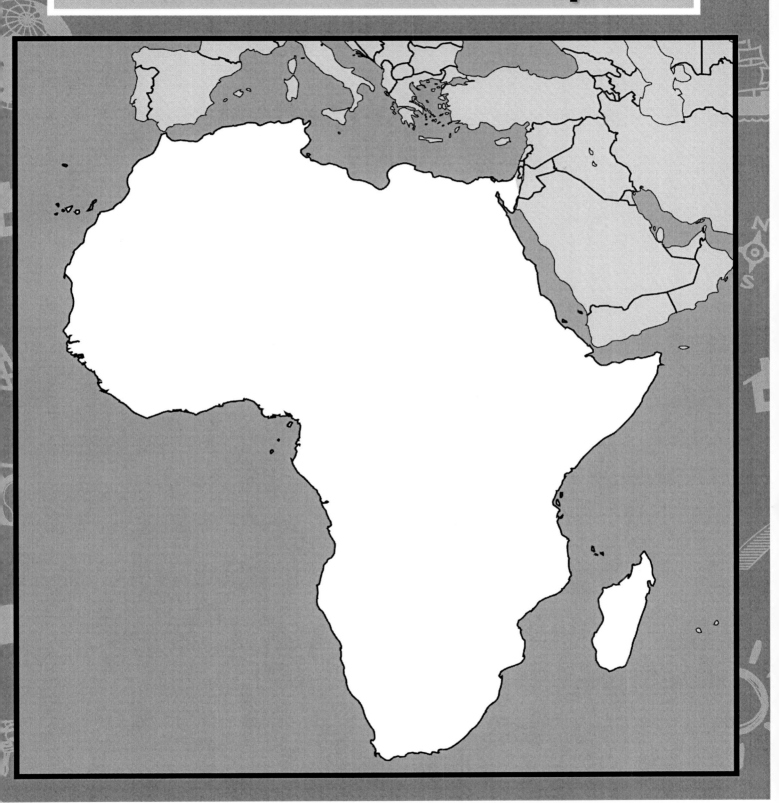

Africa CC5753

# Africa
# Western Region

# Africa
# Central Region

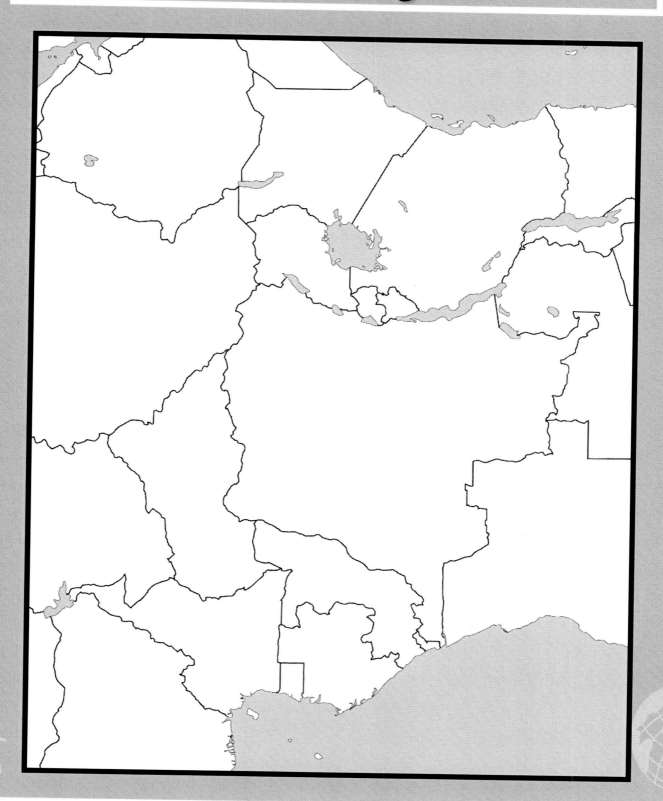

# Africa
# Southern Region

# Africa
## World Location Map

# Africa
## Globe View Map

# Africa
# Outline Map

Portugal · Spain · Italy · Bulgaria · *Black Sea* · Georgia · Azerb. · Turkmenis

Albania · Mace · Greece · Turkey · Syria · Iran

Canary Islands · Morocco · Malta · *Mediterranean Sea* · Cyprus · Lebanon · Israel · Jordan · Iraq · Kuwait · Bahrain · Qatar

Western Sahara (Occupied by Morocco) · Algeria · Libya · Egypt · Saudi Arabia · U.A.E.

**TROPIC OF CANCER**

Mali · Mauritania · *Red Sea* · Oman

Niger · Chad · Eritrea · Yemen

Gambia · Senegal · Sudan · Djibouti · Somalia

Guinea-Bissau · Burkina Faso · Ghana · Benin · Nigeria · Ethiopia

Sierra Leone · Guinea · Cote d'Ivoire · Central Africa Republic

Liberia · Cameroon · Uganda · Kenya

Equatorial Guinea · Sao Tome & Principe · Congo

**EQUATOR** · Gabon · Dem. Republic of Congo · Rwanda · Burundi

**PRIME MERIDIAN** · Tanzania · Comoros

Angola · Zambia · Mozambique · Malawi

*South* · Namibia · Zimbabwe · Madagascar · Mauri · Reunion

*Atlantic* · Botswana · **TROPIC OF CAPRICORN**

*Ocean* · Swaziland · Lesotho · South Africa

# Africa
# Physical Map

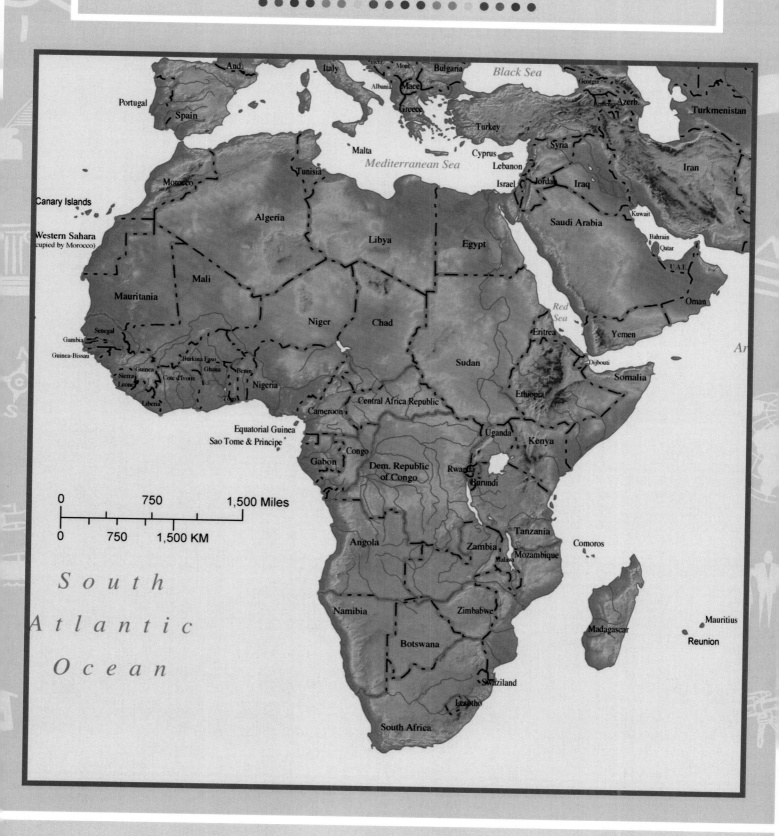

Portugal
And.
Italy
Mont.
Bulgaria
*Black Sea*
Georgia
Spain
Albania
Mace.
Armenia
Azerb.
Turkmenistan
Greece
Turkey
Malta
Cyprus
Syria
Iran
Morocco
Tunisia
*Mediterranean Sea*
Israel
Lebanon
Jordan
Iraq
Kuwait
Canary Islands
Algeria
Libya
Egypt
Saudi Arabia
Bahrain
Qatar
Western Sahara
(occupied by Morocco)
U.A.E.
Mali
Oman
Mauritania
Niger
Chad
*Red Sea*
Yemen
Gambia
Senegal
Eritrea
Guinea-Bissau
Burkina Faso
Djibouti
Sierra
Leone
Guinea
Ghana
Benin
Nigeria
Sudan
Somalia
Cote d'Ivoire
Togo
Ethiopia
Liberia
Central Africa Republic
Cameroon
Equatorial Guinea
Uganda
Kenya
Sao Tome & Principe
Congo
Gabon
Dem. Republic
of Congo
Rwanda
Burundi
Tanzania
Comoros
Angola
Zambia
Mozambique
Malawi

*S o u t h*

*A t l a n t i c*

Namibia
Zimbabwe
Mauritius
Madagascar
Reunion

*O c e a n*

Botswana

Swaziland
Lesotho
South Africa

0    750    1,500 Miles
0    750    1,500 KM

# Africa
## Major Population Map

Country
★ **National Capitals**
● Major City

# Africa
# Political Map

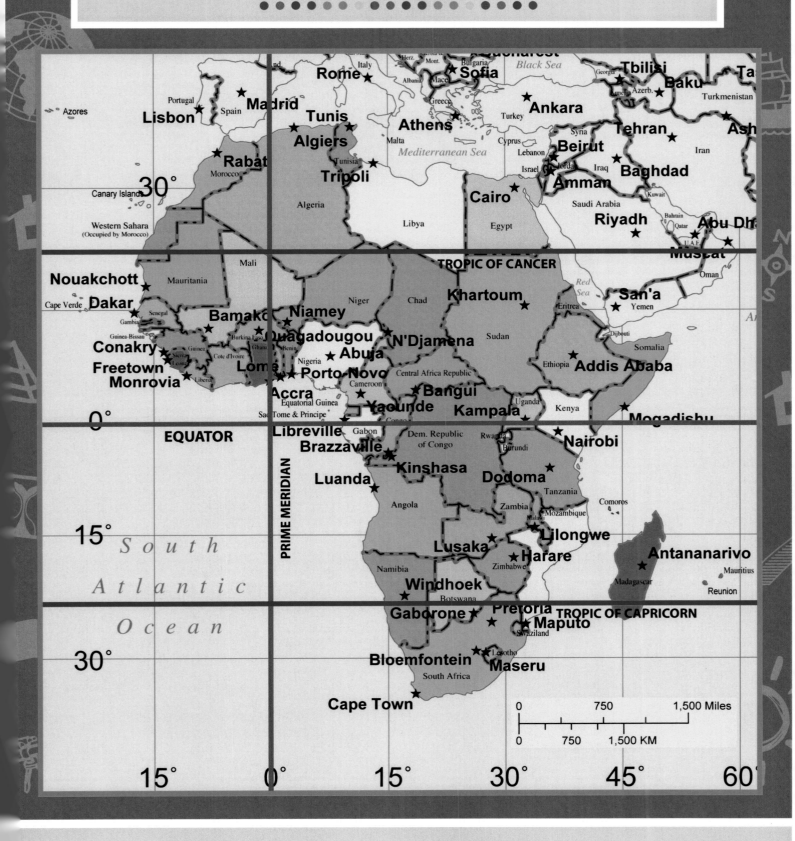

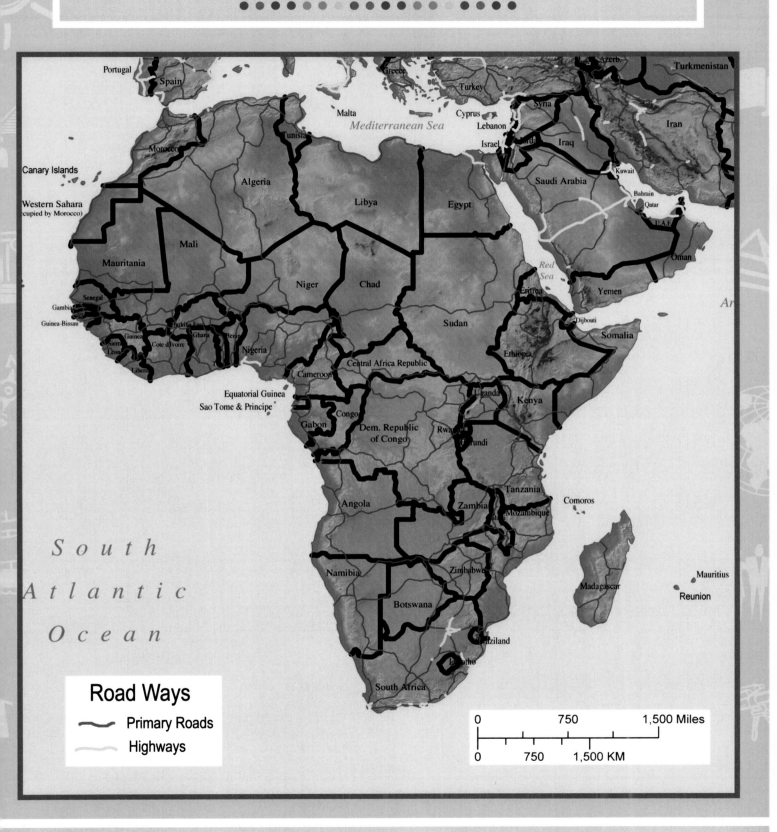

# Africa
# Transportation Map

Portugal
Spain
Greece
Turkey
Malta
Mediterranean Sea
Cyprus
Lebanon
Israel
Syria
Iraq
Iran
Turkmenistan
Azerb.

Canary Islands
Morocco
Tunisia
Algeria
Libya
Egypt
Saudi Arabia
Kuwait
Bahrain
Qatar
U.A.E.
Oman

Western Sahara
(occupied by Morocco)
Mauritania
Mali
Niger
Chad
Sudan
Red Sea
Eritrea
Yemen

Senegal
Gambia
Guinea-Bissau
Guinea
Sierra Leone
Liberia
Cote d'Ivoire
Burkina Faso
Ghana
Benin
Togo
Nigeria
Cameroon
Central Africa Republic
Equatorial Guinea
Sao Tome & Principe
Gabon
Congo
Dem. Republic of Congo
Rwanda
Burundi
Uganda
Kenya
Ethiopia
Djibouti
Somalia

Angola
Zambia
Tanzania
Mozambique
Comoros
Malawi

Namibia
Botswana
Zimbabwe
Swaziland
Lesotho
South Africa

Madagascar
Mauritius
Reunion

South Atlantic Ocean

## Road Ways
— Primary Roads
— Highways

| 0 | 750 | 1,500 Miles |
|---|-----|-------------|
| 0 | 750 | 1,500 KM |

# Africa
# Waterway Map

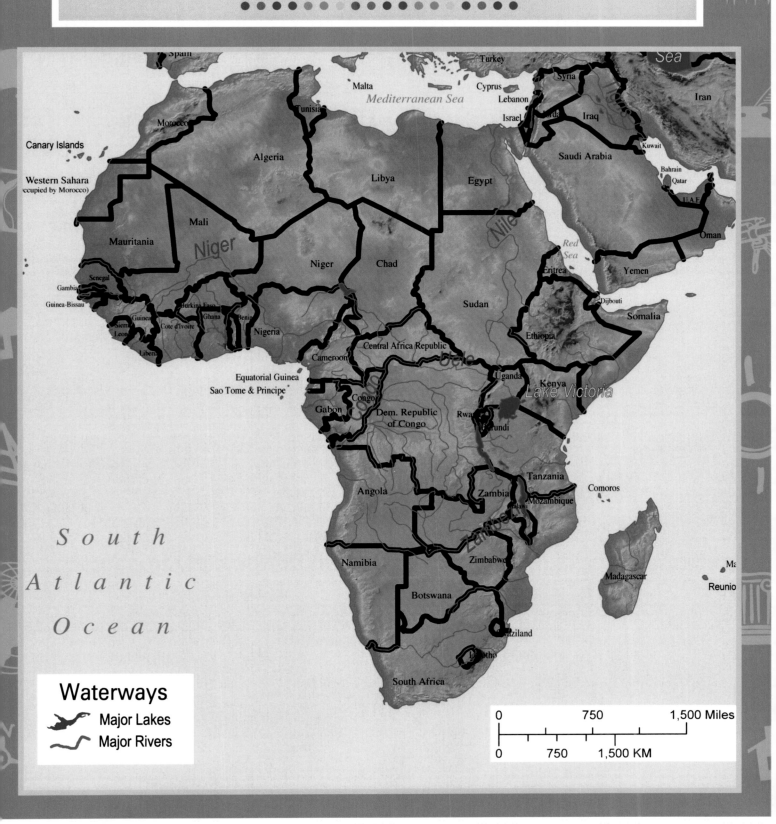

Turkey

Malta

Mediterranean Sea

Cyprus

Lebanon

Israel

Syria

Iraq

Iran

Spain

Morocco

Canary Islands

Western Sahara
(occupied by Morocco)

Mauritania

Senegal

Gambia

Guinea-Bissau

Sierra Leone

Liberia

Guinea

Cote d'Ivoire

Algeria

Mali

Niger

Burkina Faso

Ghana

Benin

Tunisia

Niger

Nigeria

Cameroon

Libya

Chad

Egypt

Sudan

Nile

Kuwait

Bahrain

Qatar

U.A.E.

Oman

Saudi Arabia

Red Sea

Eritrea

Djibouti

Somalia

Ethiopia

Yemen

Equatorial Guinea

Sao Tome & Principe

Gabon

Congo

Congo

Central Africa Republic

Dem. Republic
of Congo

Rwanda

Burundi

Uganda

Kenya

Lake Victoria

Tanzania

Comoros

Angola

Namibia

Zambia

Zambezi

Mozambique

Malawi

Zimbabwe

Botswana

Madagascar

Reunion

Swaziland

Lesotho

South Africa

South
Atlantic
Ocean

## Waterways

Major Lakes

Major Rivers

0          750          1,500 Miles

0          750          1,500 KM

# Africa
# Climate Map

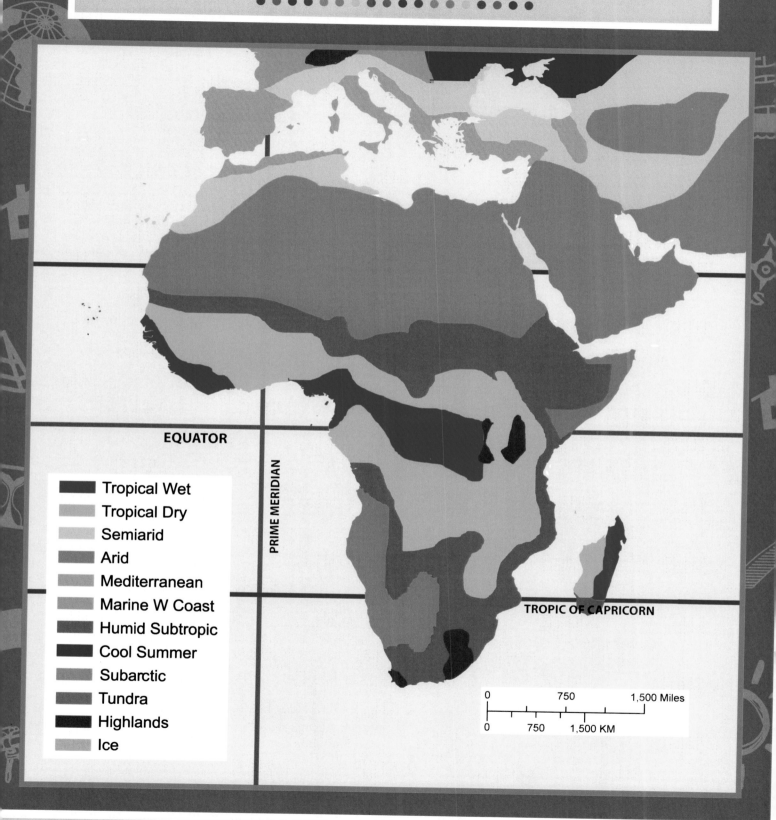

EQUATOR

PRIME MERIDIAN

TROPIC OF CAPRICORN

- Tropical Wet
- Tropical Dry
- Semiarid
- Arid
- Mediterranean
- Marine W Coast
- Humid Subtropic
- Cool Summer
- Subarctic
- Tundra
- Highlands
- Ice

| 0 | | 750 | | 1,500 Miles |
| 0 | | 750 | 1,500 KM | |

Africa  CC5753

# Africa
## Western Region

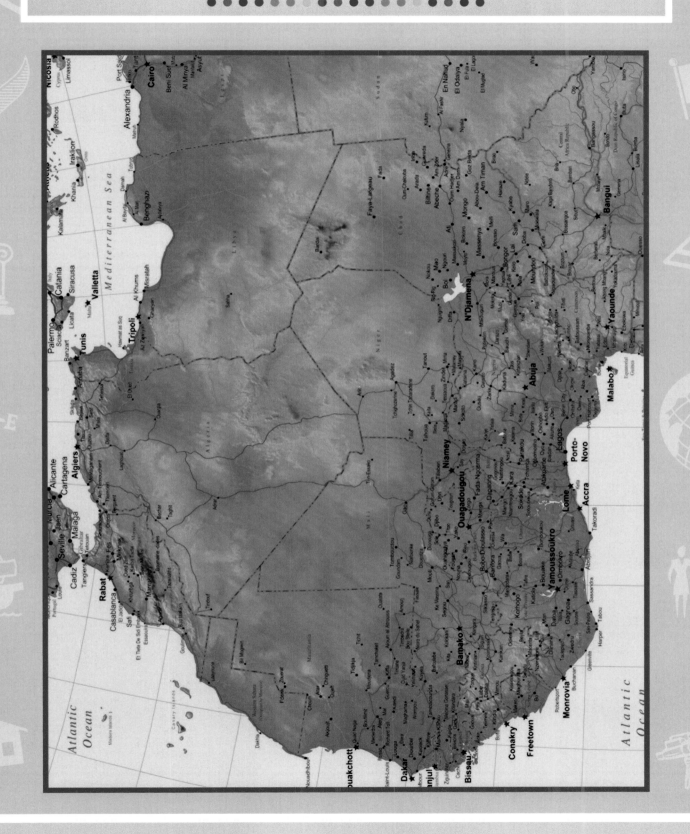

# Africa
# Central Region

Africa CC5753

# Africa
## Southern Region

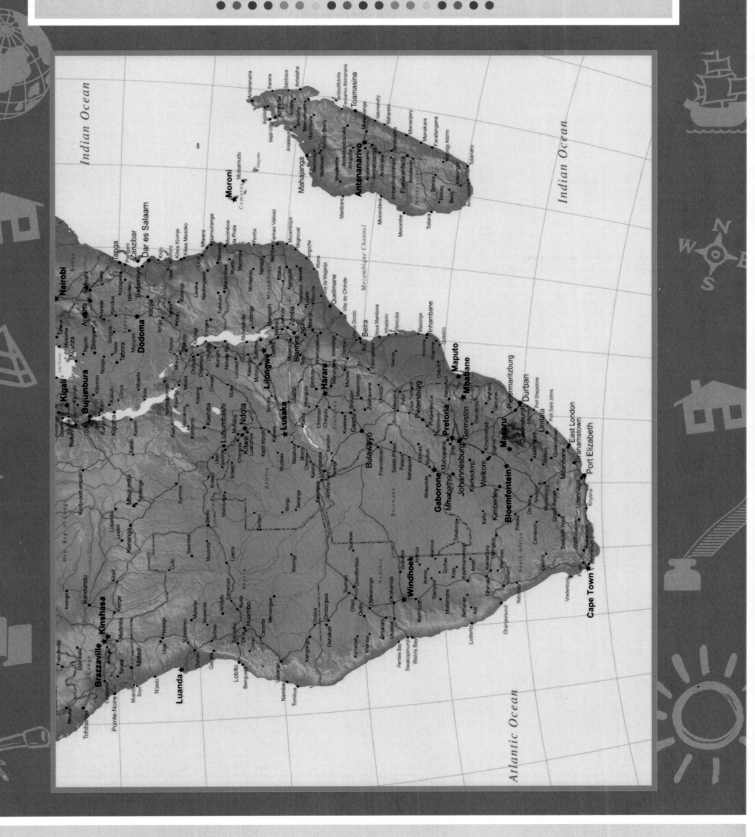

# Publication Listing
• • • • • • • • • • • • • • • • • •
## Ask Your Dealer About Our Complete Line

## SOCIAL STUDIES - Software

| ITEM # | TITLE |
|---|---|
| | **MAPPING SKILLS SERIES** |
| CC7770 | Grades PK-2 Mapping Skills with Google Earth |
| CC7771 | Grades 3-5 Mapping Skills with Google Earth |
| CC7772 | Grades 6-8 Mapping Skills with Google Earth |
| CC7773 | Grades PK-8 Mapping Skills with Google Earth Big Box |

## SOCIAL STUDIES - Books

| ITEM # | TITLE |
|---|---|
| | **MAPPING SKILLS SERIES** |
| CC5786 | Grades PK-2 Mapping Skills with Google Earth |
| CC5787 | Grades 3-5 Mapping Skills with Google Earth |
| CC5788 | Grades 6-8 Mapping Skills with Google Earth |
| CC5789 | Grades PK-8 Mapping Skills with Google Earth Big Book |
| | **NORTH AMERICAN GOVERNMENTS SERIES** |
| CC5757 | American Government |
| CC5758 | Canadian Government |
| CC5759 | Mexican Government |
| CC5760 | Governments of North America Big Book |
| | **WORLD GOVERNMENTS SERIES** |
| CC5761 | World Political Leaders |
| CC5762 | World Electoral Processes |
| CC5763 | Capitalism vs. Communism |
| CC5777 | World Politics Big Book |
| | **WORLD CONFLICT SERIES** |
| CC5511 | American Revolutionary War |
| CC5500 | American Civil War |
| CC5512 | American Wars Big Book |
| CC5501 | World War I |
| CC5502 | World War II |
| CC5503 | World Wars I & II Big Book |
| CC5505 | Korean War |
| CC5506 | Vietnam War |
| CC5507 | Korean & Vietnam Wars Big Book |
| CC5508 | Persian Gulf War (1990-1991) |
| CC5509 | Iraq War (2003-2010) |
| CC5510 | Gulf Wars Big Book |
| | **WORLD CONTINENTS SERIES** |
| CC5750 | North America |
| CC5751 | South America |
| CC5768 | The Americas Big Book |
| CC5752 | Europe |
| CC5753 | Africa |
| CC5754 | Asia |
| CC5755 | Australia |
| CC5756 | Antarctica |
| | **WORLD CONNECTIONS SERIES** |
| CC5782 | Culture, Society & Globalization |
| CC5783 | Economy & Globalization |
| CC5784 | Technology & Globalization |
| CC5785 | Globalization Big Book |

## REGULAR & REMEDIAL EDUCATION
• • • • • • • • • • • • • • •
### Reading Level 3-4  Grades 5-8

## ENVIRONMENTAL STUDIES - Software

| ITEM # | TITLE |
|---|---|
| | **CLIMATE CHANGE SERIES** |
| CC7747 | Global Warming: Causes  Grades 3-8 |
| CC7748 | Global Warming: Effects  Grades 3-8 |
| CC7749 | Global Warming: Reduction  Grades 3-8 |
| CC7750 | Global Warming Big Box  Grades 3-8 |

## ENVIRONMENTAL STUDIES - Books

| ITEM # | TITLE |
|---|---|
| | **MANAGING OUR WASTE SERIES** |
| CC5764 | Waste: At the Source |
| CC5765 | Prevention, Recycling & Conservation |
| CC5766 | Waste: The Global View |
| CC5767 | Waste Management Big Book |
| | **CLIMATE CHANGE SERIES** |
| CC5769 | Global Warming: Causes |
| CC5770 | Global Warming: Effects |
| CC5771 | Global Warming: Reduction |
| CC5772 | Global Warming Big Book |
| | **GLOBAL WATER SERIES** |
| CC5773 | Conservation: Fresh Water Resources |
| CC5774 | Conservation: Ocean Water Resources |
| CC5775 | Conservation: Waterway Habitat Resources |
| CC5776 | Water Conservation Big Book |
| | **CARBON FOOTPRINT SERIES** |
| CC5778 | Reducing Your Own Carbon Footprint |
| CC5779 | Reducing Your School's Carbon Footprint |
| CC5780 | Reducing Your Community's Carbon Footprint |
| CC5781 | Carbon Footprint Big Book |

## SCIENCE - Software

| ITEM # | TITLE |
|---|---|
| | **SPACE AND BEYOND SERIES** |
| CC7557 | Solar System Grades 5-8 |
| CC7558 | Galaxies & the Universe Grades 5-8 |
| CC7559 | Space Travel & Technology Grades 5-8 |
| CC7560 | Space Big Box Grades 5-8 |
| | **HUMAN BODY SERIES** |
| CC7549 | Cells, Skeletal & Muscular Systems  Grades 5-8 |
| CC7550 | Senses, Nervous & Respiratory Systems  Grades 5-8 |
| CC7551 | Circulatory, Digestive & Reproductive Systems  Grades 5-8 |
| CC7552 | Human Body Big Box  Grades 5-8 |
| | **FORCE, MOTION & SIMPLE MACHINES SERIES** |
| CC7553 | Force  Grades 3-8 |
| CC7554 | Motion  Grades 3-8 |
| CC7555 | Simple Machines  Grades 3-8 |
| CC7556 | Force, Motion & Simple Machines Big Box  Grades 3-8 |

## SCIENCE - Books

| ITEM # | TITLE |
|---|---|
| | **ECOLOGY & THE ENVIRONMENT SERIES** |
| CC4500 | Ecosystems |
| CC4501 | Classification & Adaptation |
| CC4502 | Cells |
| CC4503 | Ecology & The Environment Big Book |
| | **MATTER & ENERGY SERIES** |
| CC4504 | Properties of Matter |
| CC4505 | Atoms, Molecules & Elements |
| CC4506 | Energy |
| CC4507 | The Nature of Matter Big Book |
| | **FORCE & MOTION SERIES** |
| CC4508 | Force |
| CC4509 | Motion |
| CC4510 | Simple Machines |
| CC4511 | Force, Motion & Simple Machines Big Book |
| | **SPACE & BEYOND SERIES** |
| CC4512 | Solar System |
| CC4513 | Galaxies & The Universe |
| CC4514 | Travel & Technology |
| CC4515 | Space Big Book |
| | **HUMAN BODY SERIES** |
| CC4516 | Cells, Skeletal & Muscular Systems |
| CC4517 | Senses, Nervous & Respiratory Systems |
| CC4518 | Circulatory, Digestive & Reproductive Systems |
| CC4519 | Human Body Big Book |

VISIT:
### www.CLASSROOM COMPLETE PRESS.com
To view sample pages from each book

## LITERATURE KITS™ - Books

| ITEM # | TITLE |
|--------|-------|
| | **GRADES 1-2** |
| CC2100 | Curious George (H. A. Rey) |
| CC2101 | Paper Bag Princess (Robert N. Munsch) |
| CC2102 | Stone Soup (Marcia Brown) |
| CC2103 | The Very Hungry Caterpillar (Eric Carle) |
| CC2104 | Where the Wild Things Are (Maurice Sendak) |
| | **GRADES 3-4** |
| CC2300 | Babe: The Gallant Pig (Dick King-Smith) |
| CC2301 | Because of Winn-Dixie (Kate DiCamillo) |
| CC2302 | The Tale of Despereaux (Kate DiCamillo) |
| CC2303 | James and the Giant Peach (Roald Dahl) |
| CC2304 | Ramona Quimby, Age 8 (Beverly Cleary) |
| CC2305 | The Mouse and the Motorcycle (Beverly Cleary) |
| CC2306 | Charlotte's Web (E.B. White) |
| CC2307 | Owls in the Family (Farley Mowat) |
| CC2308 | Sarah, Plain and Tall (Patricia MacLachlan) |
| CC2309 | Matilda (Roald Dahl) |
| CC2310 | Charlie & The Chocolate Factory (Roald Dahl) |
| CC2311 | Frindle (Andrew Clements) |
| CC2312 | M.C. Higgins, the Great (Virginia Hamilton) |
| CC2313 | The Family Under The Bridge (N.S. Carlson) |
| CC2314 | The Hundred Penny Box (Sharon Mathis) |
| CC2315 | Cricket in Times Square (George Selden) |
| CC2316 | Fantastic Mr Fox (Roald Dahl) |
| CC2317 | The Hundred Dresses (Eleanor Estes) |
| | **GRADES 5-6** |
| CC2500 | Black Beauty (Anna Sewell) |
| CC2501 | Bridge to Terabithia (Katherine Paterson) |
| CC2502 | Bud, Not Buddy (Christopher Paul Curtis) |
| CC2503 | The Egypt Game (Zilpha Keatley Snyder) |
| CC2504 | The Great Gilly Hopkins (Katherine Paterson) |
| CC2505 | Holes (Louis Sachar) |
| CC2506 | Number the Stars (Lois Lowry) |
| CC2507 | The Sign of the Beaver (E.G. Speare) |
| CC2508 | The Whipping Boy (Sid Fleischman) |
| CC2509 | Island of the Blue Dolphins (Scott O'Dell) |
| CC2510 | Underground to Canada (Barbara Smucker) |
| CC2511 | Loser (Jerry Spinelli) |
| CC2512 | The Higher Power of Lucky (Susan Patron) |
| CC2513 | Kira-Kira (Cynthia Kadohata) |
| CC2514 | Dear Mr. Henshaw (Beverly Cleary) |
| CC2515 | The Summer of the Swans (Betsy Byars) |
| CC2516 | Shiloh (Phyllis Reynolds Naylor) |
| CC2517 | A Single Shard (Linda Sue Park) |
| CC2518 | Hoot (Carl Hiaasen) |
| CC2519 | Hatchet (Gary Paulsen) |
| CC2520 | The Giver (Lois Lowry) |
| CC2521 | The Graveyard Book (Neil Gaiman) |
| CC2522 | The View From Saturday (E.L. Konigsburg) |
| CC2523 | Hattie Big Sky (Kirby Larson) |
| CC2524 | When You Reach Me (Rebecca Stead) |
| CC2525 | Criss Cross (Lynne Rae Perkins) |
| CC2526 | A Year Down Yonder (Richard Peck) |
| CC2527 | Maniac Magee (Jerry Spinelli) |

## LITERATURE KITS™ - Books

| ITEM # | TITLE |
|--------|-------|
| CC2528 | From the Mixed-Up Files of Mrs. Basil E. Frankweiler (E.L. Konigsburg) |
| CC2529 | Sing Down the Moon (Scott O'Dell) |
| | **GRADES 7-8** |
| CC2700 | Cheaper by the Dozen (Frank B. Gilbreth) |
| CC2701 | The Miracle Worker (William Gibson) |
| CC2702 | The Red Pony (John Steinbeck) |
| CC2703 | Treasure Island (Robert Louis Stevenson) |
| CC2704 | Romeo & Juliet (William Shakespeare) |
| CC2705 | Crispin: The Cross of Lead (Avi) |
| CC2707 | The Boy in the Striped Pajamas (John Boyne) |
| CC2708 | The Westing Game (Ellen Raskin) |
| | **GRADES 9-12** |
| CC2001 | To Kill A Mockingbird (Harper Lee) |
| CC2002 | Angela's Ashes (Frank McCourt) |
| CC2003 | The Grapes of Wrath (John Steinbeck) |
| CC2004 | The Good Earth (Pearl S. Buck) |
| CC2005 | The Road (Cormac McCarthy) |
| CC2006 | The Old Man and the Sea (Ernest Hemingway) |
| CC2007 | Lord of the Flies (William Golding) |
| CC2008 | The Color Purple (Alice Walker) |
| CC2009 | The Outsiders (S.E. Hinton) |
| CC2010 | Hamlet (William Shakespeare) |
| CC2012 | The Adventures of Huckleberry Finn (Mark Twain) |
| CC2013 | Macbeth (William Shakespeare) |

## LANGUAGE ARTS - Software

| ITEM # | TITLE |
|--------|-------|
| CC7112 | **Word Families - Short Vowels Grades PK-2** |
| CC7113 | **Word Families - Long Vowels Grades PK-2** |
| CC7114 | **Word Families - Vowels Big Box Grades PK-2** |
| CC7100 | **High Frequency Sight Words  Grades PK-2** |
| CC7101 | **High Frequency Picture Words  Grades PK-2** |
| CC7102 | **Sight & Picture Words Big Box  Grades PK-2** |
| CC7104 | **How to Write a Paragraph  Grades 3-8** |
| CC7105 | **How to Write a Book Report  Grades 3-8** |
| CC7106 | **How to Write an Essay  Grades 3-8** |
| CC7107 | **Master Writing Big Box  Grades 3-8** |
| CC7108 | **Reading Comprehension  Grades 5-8** |
| CC7109 | **Literary Devices  Grades 5-8** |
| CC7110 | **Critical Thinking  Grades 5-8** |
| CC7111 | **Master Reading Big Box  Grades 5-8** |

## LANGUAGE ARTS - Books

| ITEM # | TITLE |
|--------|-------|
| CC1110 | Word Families - Short Vowels Grades K-1 |
| CC1111 | Word Families - Long Vowels Grades K-1 |
| CC1112 | Word Families - Vowels Big Book Grades K-1 |
| CC1113 | High Frequency Sight Words Grades K-1 |
| CC1114 | High Frequency Picture Words Grades K-1 |
| CC1115 | Sight & Picture Words Big Book Grades K-1 |
| CC1100 | How to Write a Paragraph  Grades 5-8 |
| CC1101 | How to Write a Book Report  Grades 5-8 |
| CC1102 | How to Write an Essay  Grades 5-8 |
| CC1103 | Master Writing Big Book  Grades 5-8 |
| CC1116 | Reading Comprehension  Grades 5-8 |
| CC1117 | Literary Devices  Grades 5-8 |
| CC1118 | Critical Thinking  Grades 5-8 |
| CC1119 | Master Reading Big Book  Grades 5-8 |
| CC1106 | Reading Response Forms: Grades 1-2 |
| CC1107 | Reading Response Forms: Grades 3-4 |
| CC1108 | Reading Response Forms: Grades 5-6 |
| CC1109 | Reading Response Forms Big Book: Grades 1-6 |

## MATHEMATICS - Software

| ITEM # | TITLE |
|--------|-------|
| | **PRINCIPLES & STANDARDS OF MATH SERIES** |
| CC7315 | Grades PK-2 Five Strands of Math Big Box |
| CC7316 | Grades 3-5 Five Strands of Math Big Box |
| CC7317 | Grades 6-8 Five Strands of Math Big Box |

## MATHEMATICS - Books

| | |
|--------|-------|
| | **TASK SHEETS** |
| CC3100 | Grades PK-2 Number & Operations Task Sheets |
| CC3101 | Grades PK-2 Algebra Task Sheets |
| CC3102 | Grades PK-2 Geometry Task Sheets |
| CC3103 | Grades PK-2 Measurement Task Sheets |
| CC3104 | Grades PK-2 Data Analysis & Probability Task Sheets |
| CC3105 | Grades PK-2 Five Strands of Math Big Book Task Sheets |
| CC3106 | Grades 3-5 Number & Operations Task Sheets |
| CC3107 | Grades 3-5 Algebra Task Sheets |
| CC3108 | Grades 3-5 Geometry Task Sheets |
| CC3109 | Grades 3-5 Measurement Task Sheets |
| CC3110 | Grades 3-5 Data Analysis & Probability Task Sheets |
| CC3111 | Grades 3-5 Five Strands of Math Big Book Task Sheets |
| CC3112 | Grades 6-8 Number & Operations Task Sheets |
| CC3113 | Grades 6-8 Algebra Task Sheets |
| CC3114 | Grades 6-8 Geometry Task Sheets |
| CC3115 | Grades 6-8 Measurement Task Sheets |
| CC3116 | Grades 6-8 Data Analysis & Probability Task Sheets |
| CC3117 | Grades 6-8 Five Strands of Math Big Book Task Sheets |
| | **DRILL SHEETS** |
| CC3200 | Grades PK-2 Number & Operations Drill Sheets |
| CC3201 | Grades PK-2 Algebra Drill Sheets |
| CC3202 | Grades PK-2 Geometry Drill Sheets |
| CC3203 | Grades PK-2 Measurement Drill Sheets |
| CC3204 | Grades PK-2 Data Analysis & Probability Drill Sheets |
| CC3205 | Grades PK-2 Five Strands of Math Big Book Drill Sheets |
| CC3206 | Grades 3-5 Number & Operations Drill Sheets |
| CC3207 | Grades 3-5 Algebra Drill Sheets |
| CC3208 | Grades 3-5 Geometry Drill Sheets |
| CC3209 | Grades 3-5 Measurement Drill Sheets |
| CC3210 | Grades 3-5 Data Analysis & Probability Drill Sheets |
| CC3211 | Grades 3-5 Five Strands of Math Big Book Drill Sheets |
| CC3212 | Grades 6-8 Number & Operations Drill Sheets |
| CC3213 | Grades 6-8 Algebra Drill Sheets |
| CC3214 | Grades 6-8 Geometry Drill Sheets |
| CC3215 | Grades 6-8 Measurement Drill Sheets |
| CC3216 | Grades 6-8 Data Analysis & Probability Drill Sheets |
| CC3217 | Grades 6-8 Five Strands of Math Big Book Drill Sheets |
| | **TASK & DRILL SHEETS** |
| CC3300 | Grades PK-2 Number & Operations Task & Drill Sheets |
| CC3301 | Grades PK-2 Algebra Task & Drill Sheets |
| CC3302 | Grades PK-2 Geometry Task & Drill Sheets |
| CC3303 | Grades PK-2 Measurement Task & Drill Sheets |
| CC3304 | Grades PK-2 Data Analysis & Probability Task & Drills |
| CC3306 | Grades 3-5 Number & Operations Task & Drill Sheets |
| CC3307 | Grades 3-5 Algebra Task & Drill Sheets |
| CC3308 | Grades 3-5 Geometry Task & Drill Sheets |
| CC3309 | Grades 3-5 Measurement Task & Drill Sheets |
| CC3310 | Grades 3-5 Data Analysis & Probability Task & Drills |
| CC3312 | Grades 6-8 Number & Operations Task & Drill Sheets |
| CC3313 | Grades 6-8 Algebra Task & Drill Sheets |
| CC3314 | Grades 6-8 Geometry Task & Drill Sheets |
| CC3315 | Grades 6-8 Measurement Task & Drill Sheets |
| CC3316 | Grades 6-8 Data Analysis & Probability Task & Drills |